Preface

This book is in no way offering a risk-free trading method in the Forex market.

The profession of trader itself is a risky profession, and risk management is an important pillar in the success of your transactions.

This book will provide you with a good understanding of the Forex market and the most important tools available to traders. It will also provide you with the opportunity to learn how to analyse chart patterns as most of the graphs have chart patterns that can be determined in advance.

This book will help you develop your analytical skills to better inform your decisions of buying and selling.

Finally, it is worth it to mention that if applied correctly, and if risks and stops are respected, the method described in this book will offer you a success rate of up to 80%.

<u>Warning</u>

This trading book does not engage my responsibility in any way with an obligation of result. I am committed to providing you with the technical tools necessary to succeed in the Forex space. However, the forex market like any other financial market, has its own risks. Rigor, common sense and deep analysis are required in order to avoid losses.

Thus, I decline all legal responsibilities with regard to the expected results as these will vary according to your level of understanding of the tools described and according to the reduction of losses with regard to losing delays.

As a final note, your questions and feedback are always welcome. Please leave me a comment and I will revert back to you as soon as possible with an answer.

TABLE OF CONTENTS

INTRODUCTION : 4

Part I 5

Presentation of the Forex space, the Meta Trader 4 trading platform and presentation of the Ichimoku technique as well as the strong buy and sell signals 5

   1. Presentation of the Forex space and the Meta Trader 4 trading platform 6

      a) Definition and presentation of the Forex market: 6
      b) The Meta Trader 4 trading platform : 7

   3. Presentation of analysis tools and the strong buy & sell signals : 7

      a) Overview of Ichimoku Kinko Hyo 7
      b) Ichimoku on a graph : 9
      c) Bearish Ichimoku signals: 13
      d) Ichimoku bullish signals: 15

PART II 17

Presentation of the RSI, moving averages, the most common chart figures as well as their analyses and buy and sell decisions according to the accumulation of indicators related to the method. 17

   1) Presentation of the RSI and the moving averages method as well as the most common chartist figures: 18

      a) The RSI (see graph n°7) 18
      b) Moving averages : 19
      c) The most famous chartist figures : 22

   2) Purchase and sale decisions following the accumulation of indicators linked to the method (global strategy) 27

      a) Use of Ichimoku, RSI and figures chartists : 27
      b) Use of moving averages and RSI : 31

CONCLUSION : 32

INTRODUCTION :

This guide for new traders is a complete training, which will allow you to become financially independent and succeed in most of your Forex transactions.

To understand the strategy adopted in this book, we will discuss two fundamental chapters:

1. Presentation of the Forex space, the Meta Trader 4 trading platform and presentation of the Ichimoku technique as well as the strong buy and sell signals.
2. Presentation of the RSI, the most common chart figures as well as their analysis and the buying and selling decisions according to the accumulation of indicators related to the method.

Part I

Presentation of the Forex space, the Meta Trader 4 trading platform and presentation of the Ichimoku technique as well as the strong buy and sell signals

1. Presentation of the Forex space and the Meta Trader 4 trading platform

a) Definition and presentation of the Forex market:

The Forex is a market where the supply and demand of a currency pair collide.

When a currency appreciates against another (i.e. either because its demand has increased or due to changes in the economic situation) this constitutes a variation in the currency pairs (example: Euro/USD or USD/Canadian dollar etc…)

This is precisely the purpose of trading, to predict how one currency will evolve against another and this is by deploying technical indicators, charts and economic conditions.

Generally speaking, if the economic indicators support a decision to buy or sell and the economic situation and macroeconomic indicators give contradictory information. The decision to trade should never be taken because this contradictory information will have a much greater power than the tools used.

Important: to trade on the Forex market, you will need to choose a Broker and a trading platform.

The broker will be the intermediary between you and the market. It is thanks to the broker that you will be able to make your transactions, buy or sell a currency pair, for a commission the broker will take on your transactions and which varies depending on which broker you have chosen.

We cannot make a recommendation regarding the choice of your broker, but some of them are specialised in the Forex market.

However, I suggest that you visit the FMA "Financial Markets Authority" website where you will find a list of brokers that are blacklisted and therefore not authorised to trade in Forex. This will prevent you from failing into scam.

On the other hand for trading platforms, I could recommend Meta Trader 4 and I recommend a trading account with low leverage (for less risk).

b) **The Meta Trader 4 trading platform :**

This platform is the best known and most used in the world of Forex. It's easy and convenient, it has all the tools we will talk about and it's a free platform. You can also have a demo account to practice making transactions.

During this training, we will not learn how to use the Meta Trader 4 platform as the guidelines to do so are available on the internet and it is very easy to understand.

We will however, see how to use the analysis tools, how to configure them and how to analyse chart patterns to take stock and to take a buy or sell position.

3. **Presentation of analysis tools and the strong buy & sell signals :**
    a) **Overview of Ichimoku Kinko Hyo**

This method developed in the 20th century by the journalist Goichi Hosoda, which means in Japanese "at a glance", is a complete trading system, which is based on five key indicators that we will detail:

The Kinjun-Sen: It is a curve that retraces the average between the highest and lowest value of the last 26 periods (and this will depend on the temporality used in trading, so it will be either over the last 26 "15 minutes" or last 26 "hours" etc…) this is the blue curve on graph n°1.

The Tenkan-Sen: It is a curve that traces, similarly to Kinjun-Sen, the average between the highest and the lowest value, but this time over the last 9 periods (depending of course on the chosen temporality). Red curve on graph n°1.

Senkoun Span A: This is the average of the Tenkan and Kinjun projected over a prediction of 26 periods ahead.

The Senkoun Span B: this is the value of the average of the high and low of 52 periods including 26 periods shifted forward (prediction)

Note: the area between Senkoun Span A and Senkoun Span B is called the Ichimoku cloud, it is the place of balance between supply and demand. You should never take a buy or sell position when you are inside the Ichomoku cloud.

La Chikou: it corresponds to the closing price projected over 26 periods backwards. This is an important indicator, it is from this indicator that we will define the supports and resistances.

Supports: these are the low points where the market is expected to eventually rebound higher once they are hit.

Resistances: these are represented by the points at the top of the curve where the market is predicted to come down once it is hit.

b) Ichimoku on a graph :

- How to configure Ichimoku? :

On Meta Trader 4 you have to click on insertion, indicator and then trend indicator. Configure the graph as shown below:

Ichimoku Kinko Hyo	? ×
Parameters Colors Visualization	
Tenkan-sen: 9	
Kijun-sen: 26	
Senkou Span B: 52	
OK Annuler Reset	

The graph will appear as below : (Graph n°1) :

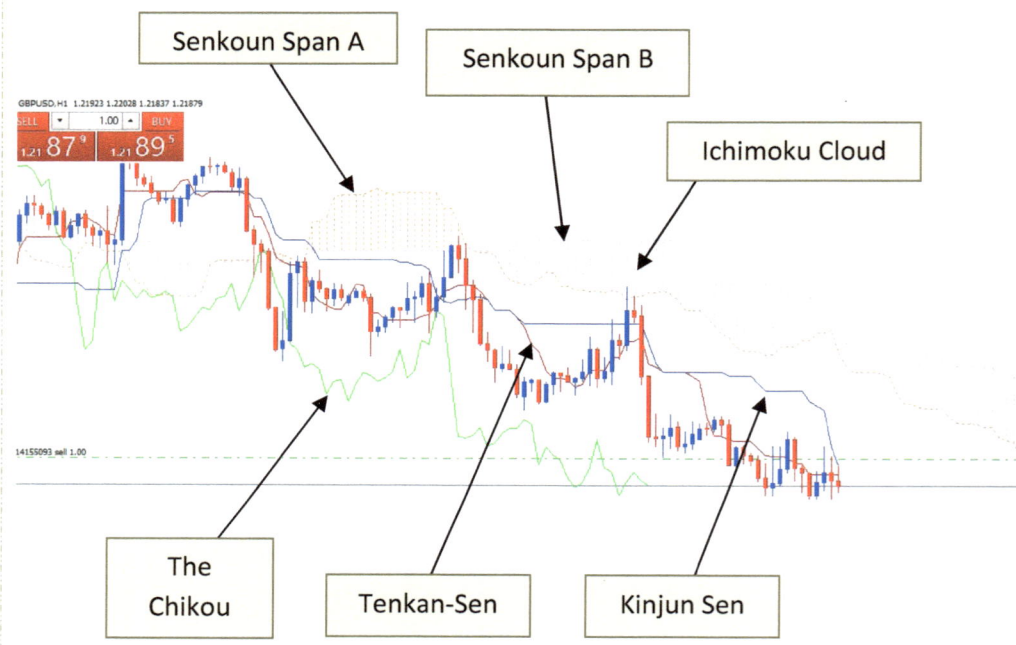

- How to delimit the supports and resistances from the Chikou ? (see graphs n°2 and n°3)

To succeed in your trades, you must know how to let your gains run and stop your losses quickly.

Support and resistances will tell us precisely when to take our gains and when to stop our losses if we are wrong. The results of 100 winning trades is not possible. But if we know how to manage risk and if we know HOW to follow the process to the letter, our gains will be greater and our loses reduced.

This Chart shows the supports : (Chart n°2):

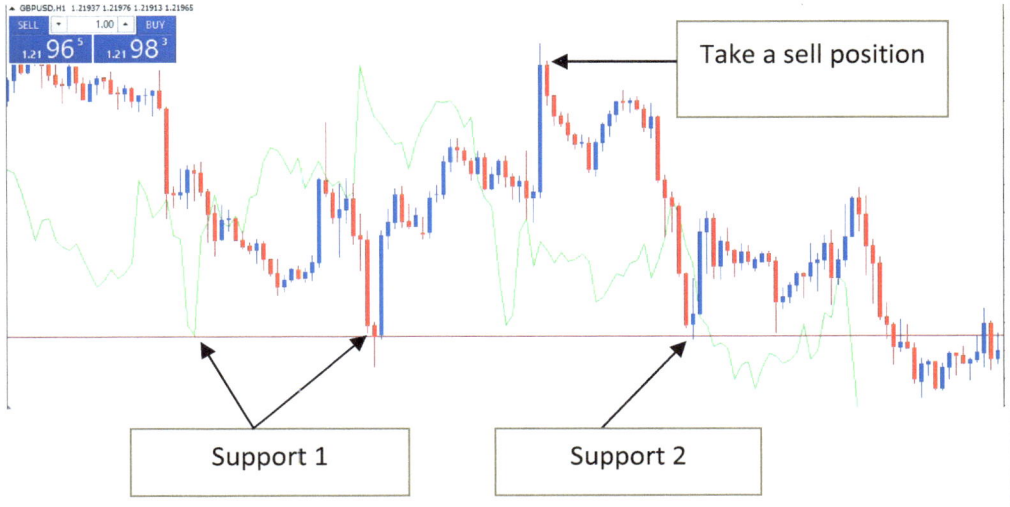

We notice on this chart that the support line that we have drawn thanks to the bottom of the Chikou, was hit by the market a second time (support 2) and hence, it was the right time to close our position if we had created our sell order higher. On this support the market rebounded upwards, in the same way it would be the right time to buy and sell higher.

Note: We do not just rely on supports and resistances to trade, we have to combine these with other indicators that we will see later.

The below graph shows resistances (Chart n°2):

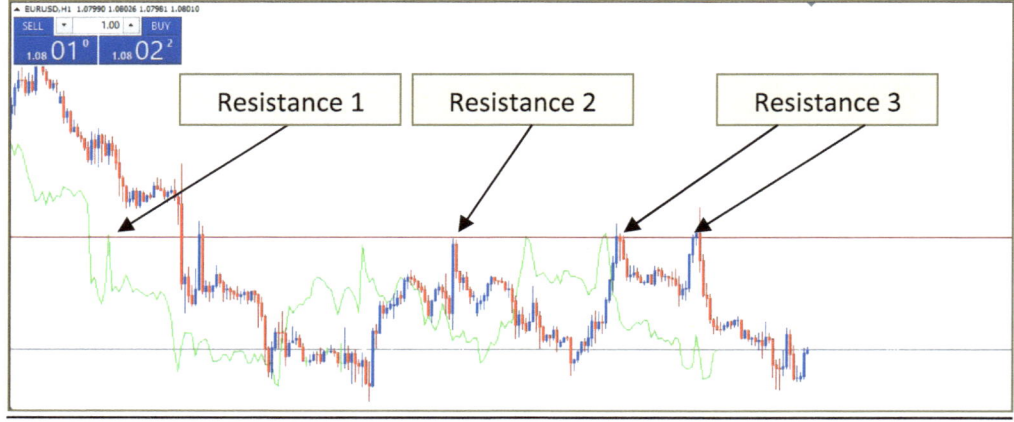

We can see the sharp top of the Chikou has allowed us to trace resistance, i.e. a high point that is difficult for the market to break through. So this resistance was hit 3 times by the market and we could position ourselves at the top of the resistance on sale and close the position at the lowest, on the supports we have chosen.

Note: In general, we create a sell order on resistance when we expect a decrease, and we close the position on the defined supports.

And in the same way we buy at the level of the supports, when we foresee an increase and we close our position on the resistances.

c) **Bearish Ichimoku signals:**

The strong bearish signal: (chart n°3)

The Chikou curve is below the Ichomoku cloud and the price. The price is crossing Senkoun Span B on the downside and we have a downward crossing between Tenkan and Kinjun.

All of these three elements give a strong bearish Signal.

The chart below shows the strong Ichimoku bearish signals (Chart n°3):

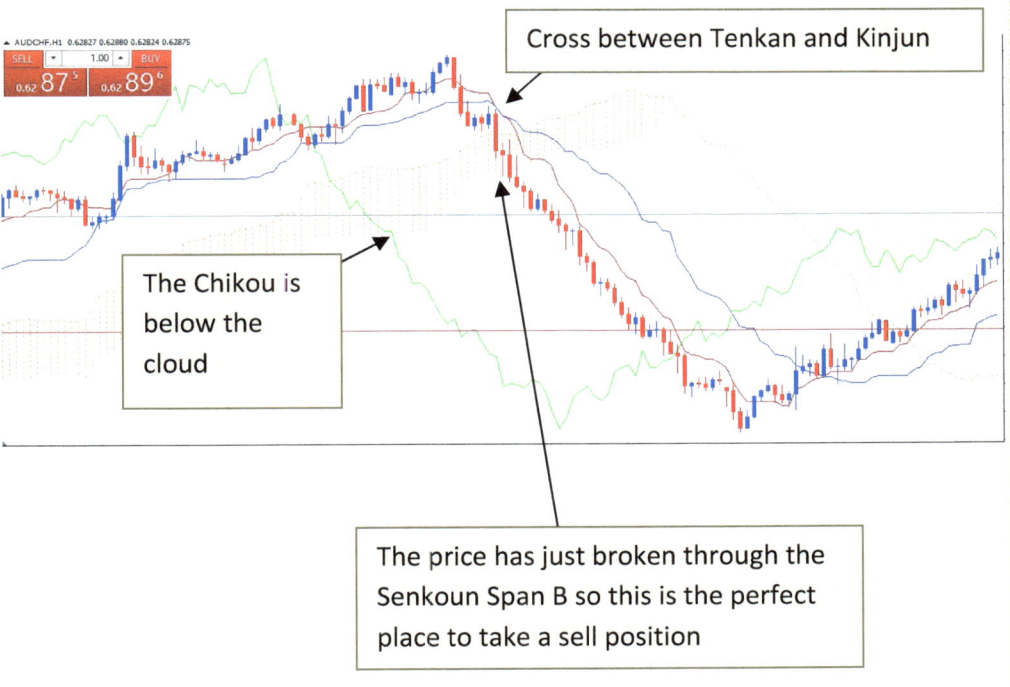

The graph shows where to position yourself to make a sell order. You have to close your position on the support that will be defined by looking at the Chikou curve over the previous period.

The average bearish signal (Chart n°4)

The price is above the Ichimoku cloud but we have a downward cross between Kinjun and Tenkan, the price crosses the Kinjun on the downside and the Chikou crosses on the downside the Tenkan and the Kinjun.

All of these indicators will give an average signal, which is to say quite likely that the market is falling.

The chart below show the average bearish Ichimoku signals (chart n°4):

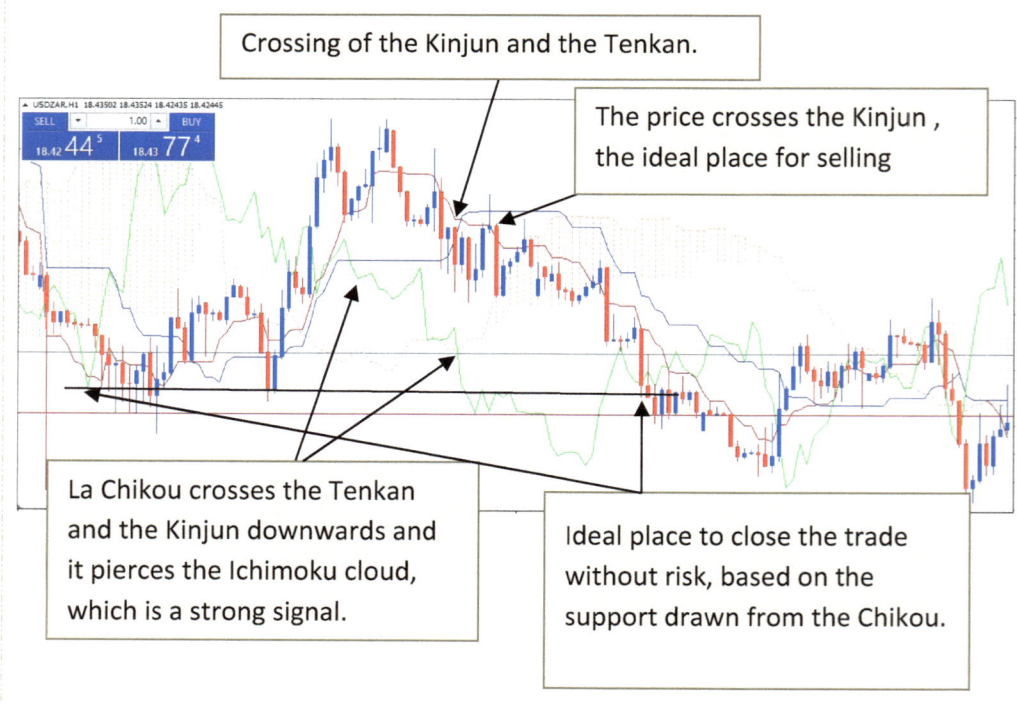

We thus see on the chart, the moment when we must enter a sell position and the moment when we must exit (at the support level). But this is only based on the Ichimoku model. We will detail other tools later and the final strategy will be based on a combination of all the tools.

d) <u>Ichimoku bullish signals</u>:

<u>The strong bullish signal</u> :

The price is above the Ichimoku cloud, the Chikou is also above the cloud and the price. We have an upward cross between Tenkan and Kinjun and the price crosses upward on the Senkou Span B (SSB). (See graph n°5)

The graph below shows strong bullish signals of Ichimoku (graph n°5)

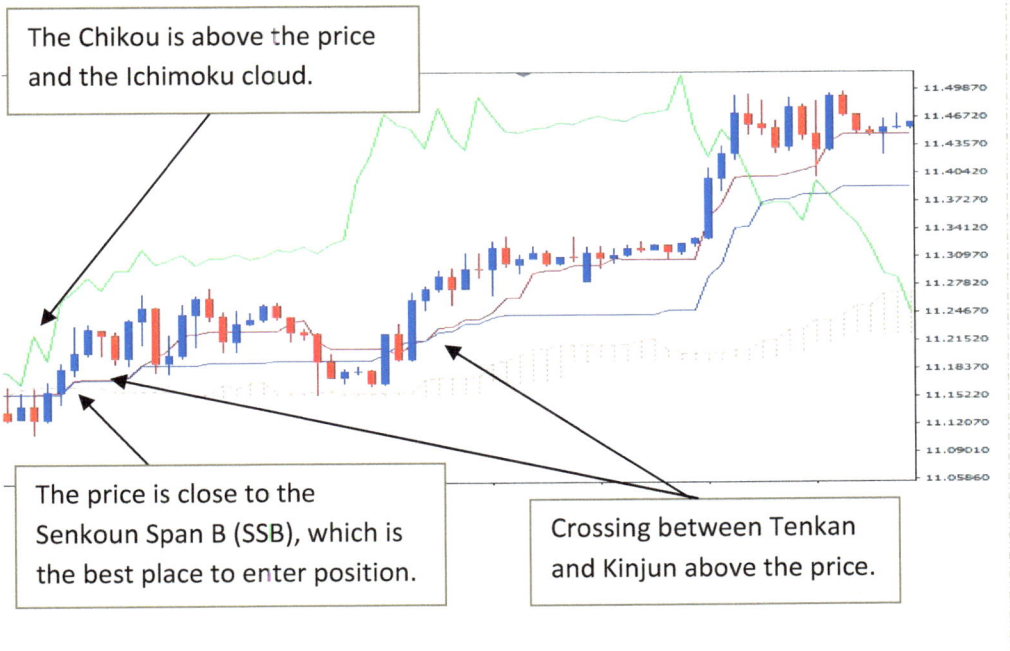

We thus notice on this graph that the best place to invest was the crossing of the price with the Senkoun Span B as we had all the signals to enter in position, a Chikou above the price and the Ichimoku cloud is a cross between Tenkan and Kinjun, also above the price.

The average Bullish signal :

The average bullish signal is a set of indicators that also gives a buy signal, but with an average accuracy. That is, there is a low risk of not being right.

The price is below the Ichimoku clouds, but we have a cross between Tenken and Kinjun on the rise. The price crosses the Kinjun and the Chikou can pierce the Tenken and the Kinjun in some cases. (See graph n°6)

PART II

Presentation of the RSI, moving averages, the most common chart figures as well as their analyses and buy and sell decisions according to the accumulation of indicators related to the method.

1) **Presentation of the RSI and the moving averages method as well as the most common chartist figures:**

   a) **The RSI (see graph n°7)**

The RSI or Relative Strength Index is an indicator that interprets the strength of the trend. When the RSI curve comes from the bottom and breaks through the 50% threshold, we are clearly in an upward trend. When the curve reaches 70% it means that the trend is likely to change (you have to be careful!)

Then when the RSI curve comes from the top and breaks through the 50% threshold, we are clearly in a downward trend, and when the curve hits 30%, the downward trend may change (so be careful here as well!).

We can combine RSI and moving averages as part of a second strategy.

We will then see the accumulation of indicators as part of a practical case, explaining the overall strategy.

The below chart that shows the average bullish Ichimoku signals (Chart n°7) :

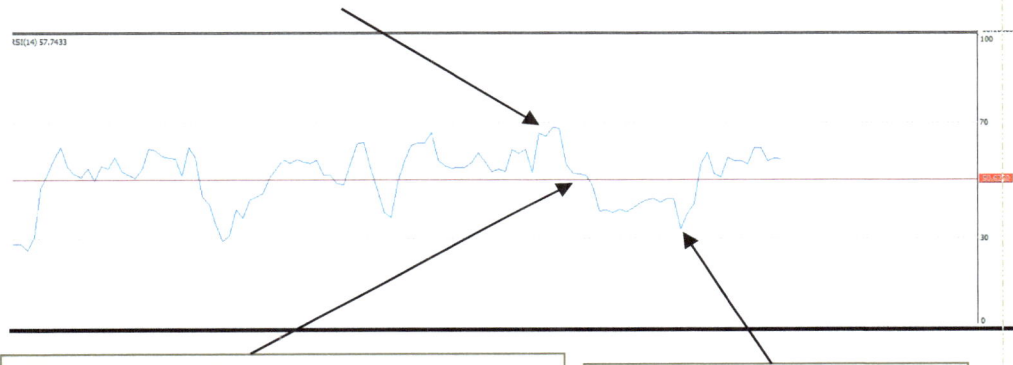

We see that the RSI curve has almost hit 70% and it has started to come down. It was the best time to position yourself in sales.

The RSI has broken through the 50% threshold, so you need to safely close your sell position because from the 30% threshold the curve may rebound, that is to say the trend will change.

The RSI hits 30% threshold, trend was likely to change and it has indeed changed.

b) **Moving averages :**

Trading with moving averages is also well known. It is a curve plotting the average closing price over different time periods.

We are going to work with three moving averages:

- A five period moving average in black (will only be used to see if there is volatility, as this curve will be very close to the price).
- A moving average over 50 periods in red.
- A moving average over 200 periods in purple.

On Meta Trader 4 you have to click on insertion, indicator, trend, moving average and you have to choose the period.

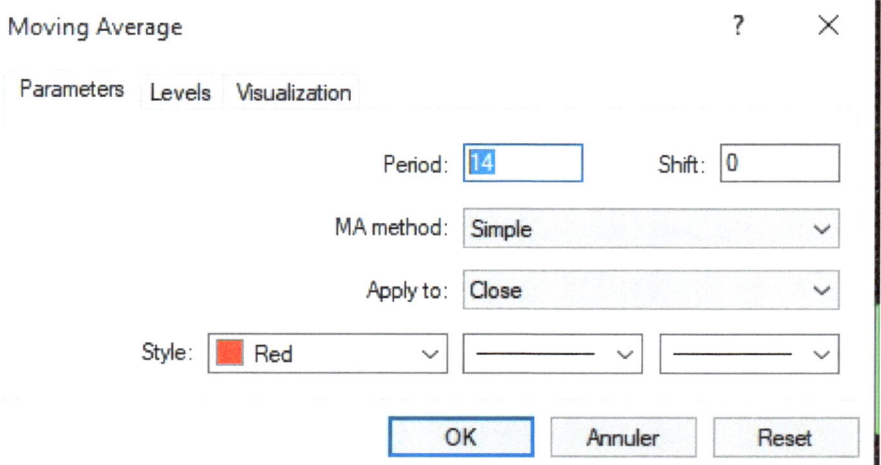

When to trade bearish with moving averages?:

We will open a short position (therefore downwards), when the price hits the 50 moving average and the two 50 and 200 moving averages will be above the price (see chart n°8 below)

The price is below the 50 period moving average and is hitting the 200 period moving average. Now is the right time to position yourself in selling. It is necessary to close on the support.

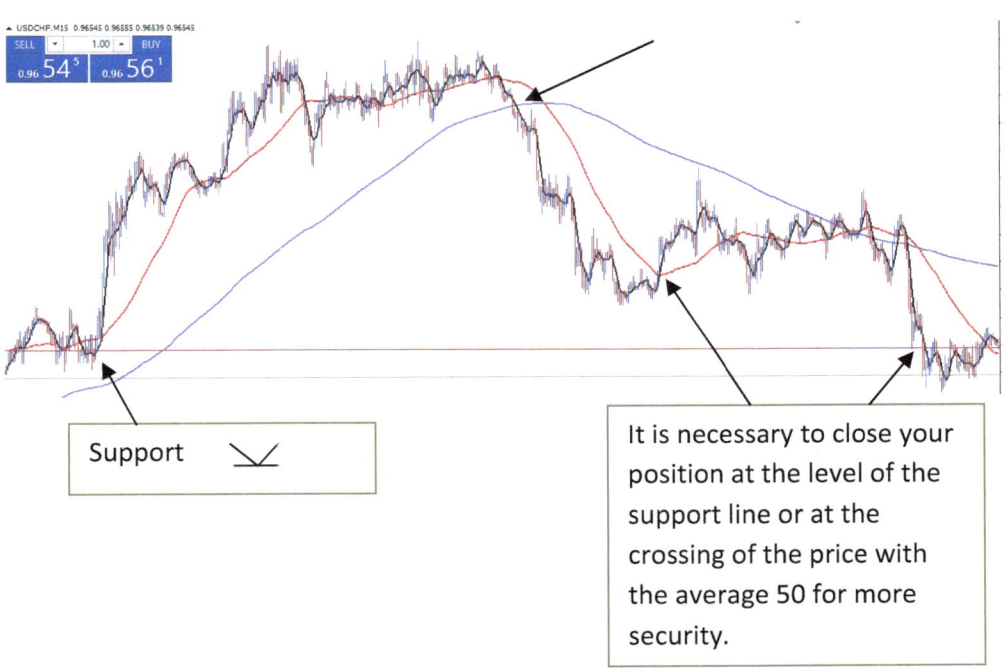

Support

It is necessary to close your position at the level of the support line or at the crossing of the price with the average 50 for more security.

When to trade bearish with moving averages? :

We will trade upward (therefore make a buying decision), when the price hits the 50 period average curve and the two 50 period and 200 period average curves will be below the price (see graph n°9 below):

c) The most famous chartist figures :

A chartist figure is a graphic configuration that is repeated on the financial markets and therefore of which we can guess the evolution. It provides you with information that is as reliable as technical indicators. Below are the most important figures:

- **Shoulder – Head – Shoulder :**

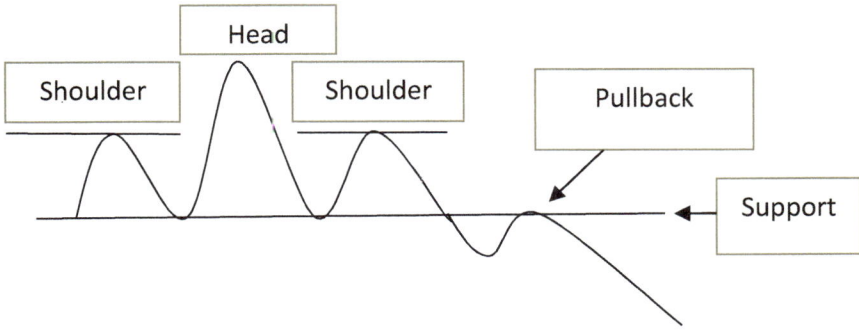

In this figure the price will come to hit the resistance at the level of the shoulder then it will come to hit the support, go up and hit a new higher resistance (the head) and at the end it will come back to the resistance to come out down (pullback). Now is the perfect time to make a selling decision.

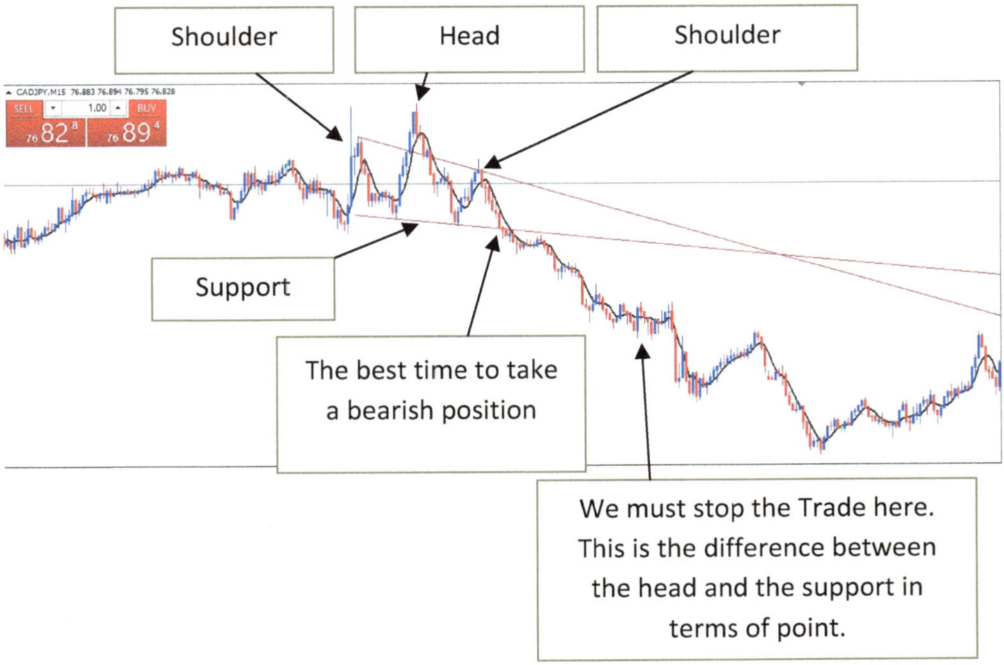

Note :

To know when to close your trade position, it's simple: it's the difference between the head and the support in Pips (point of difference).

The shoulder-head-shoulder pattern also exists in reverse order, and in this case we will make a buy decision at the shoulder breakout with resistance.

The double Top and double Bottom:

In this chart setup, the bearish signal will be given when the price hits two identical resistances points and breaks through the support down and becomes a new resistance, like this one below :

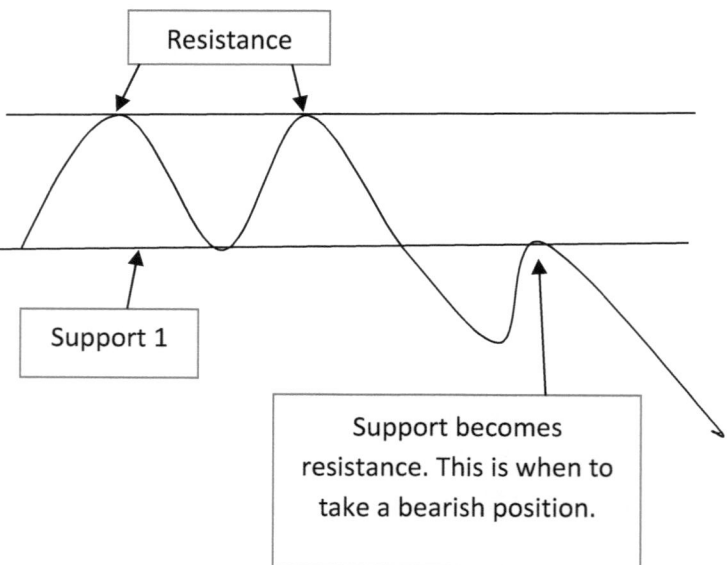

The bullish signal will be given when the price hits two identical support points and breaks through resistance upwards and becomes the new support, like this one below:

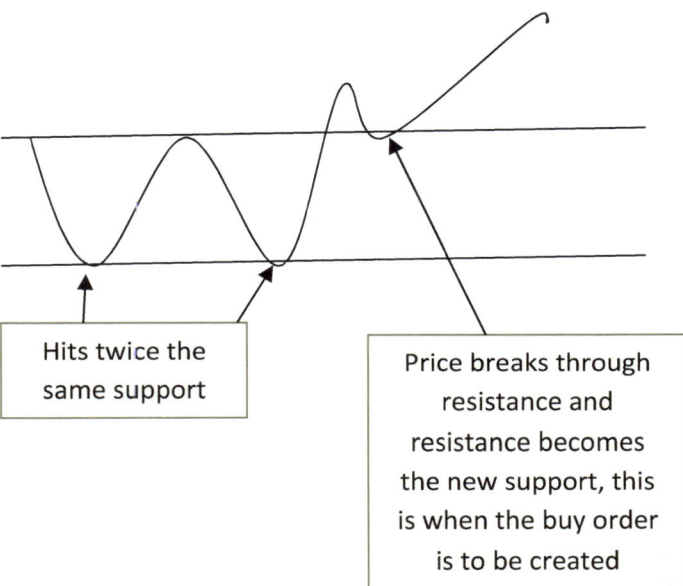

This is a graphic example of a double bottom.

The ascending and descending bevel :

The ascending wedge is a graphic configuration where the price will hit at least twice the same resistance and will hit 3 low points (support), higher than the previous ones.

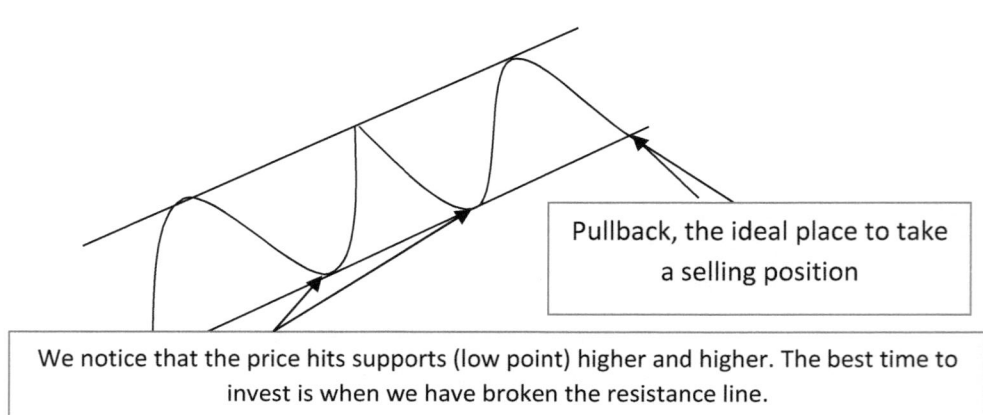

Pullback, the ideal place to take a selling position

We notice that the price hits supports (low point) higher and higher. The best time to invest is when we have broken the resistance line.

The downward wedge, meanwhile, is a graphic configuration where the price will hit at least twice the same support and will hit 3 high points (resistance), lower than the previous ones. A decision to buy must be made when the price has crossed the resistance line.

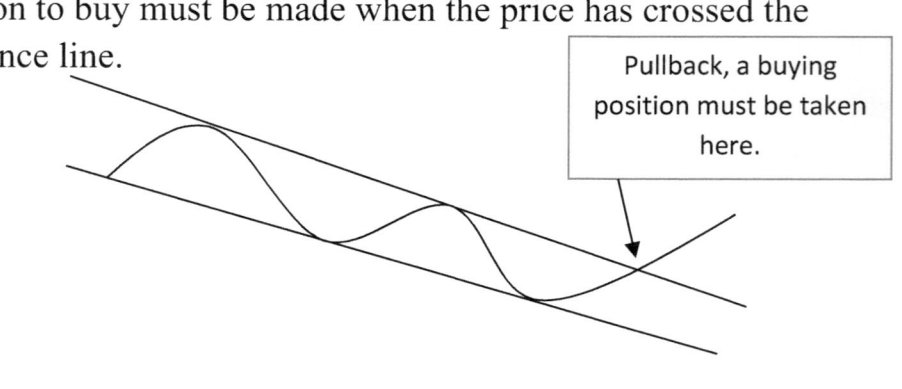

Pullback, a buying position must be taken here.

Graphically, this how an ascending bevel will translate :

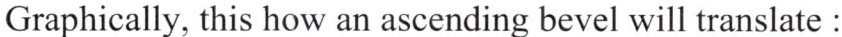

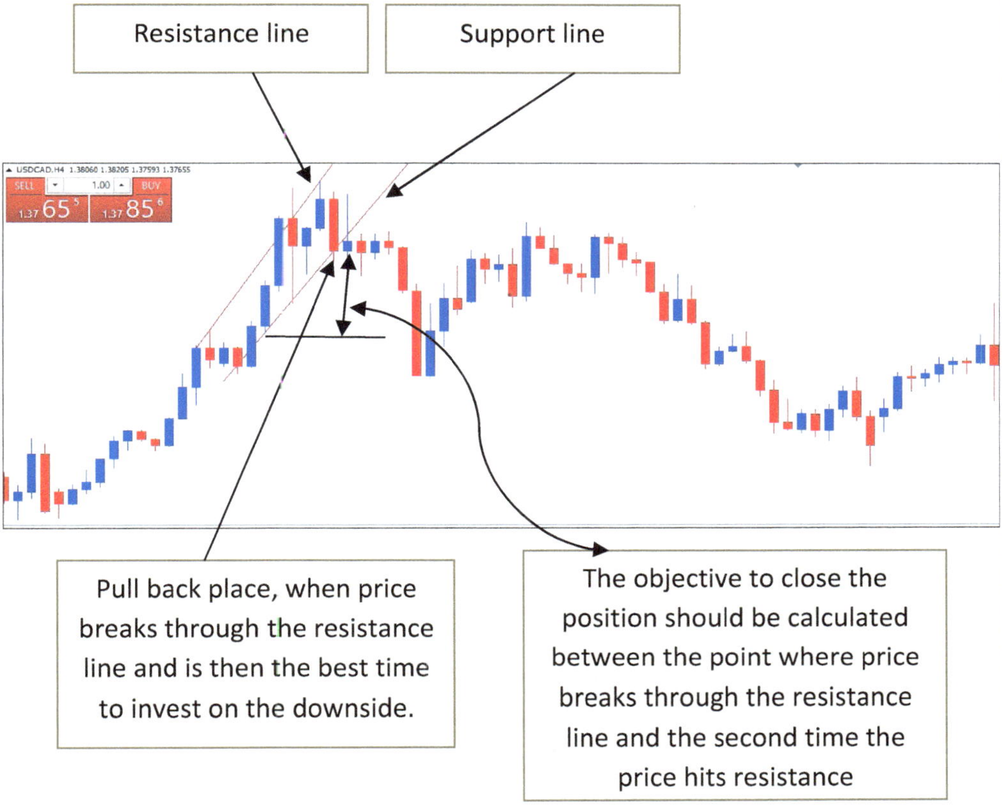
Resistance line
Support line
USDCAD,H4 1.38060 1.38205 1.37593 1.37655
SELL
1.00
BUY
Pull back place, when price breaks through the resistance line and is then the best time to invest on the downside.
The objective to close the position should be calculated between the point where price breaks through the resistance line and the second time the price hits resistance

2) Purchase and sale decisions following the accumulation of indicators linked to the method (global strategy)

a) Use of Ichimoku, RSI and figures chartists :

The strategy consists in taking a position when all the indicators give us the signal. If we trade over a time frame of 30 minutes, we must analyse the Ichimoku indicator over a time frame of one week to see if we are on an upward or downward trend then we must validate the buy or sell signals on the time frame of 1 day, 4 hours, 1 hour and then 30 minutes. So we will take a position only if all the temporalities agree to give the same Ichimoku signal to buy or sell.

Then once we have the signal, we have to check the RSI, and this is to see if we are overbought or oversold. Under no circumstances should the RSI be greater than 70% if we are to take a long position and it should not be less than 30% if we are to sell.

The RSI curve will therefore give an additional indication of the price situation (see chapter on RSI).

The third and last thing is the identification of the chartist figure. Although it is not always obvious, if we can recognise a chartist figure, it will provide us with additional credibility to the decision to buy and sell.

Practical Case (Trade of May 28th, 2020):

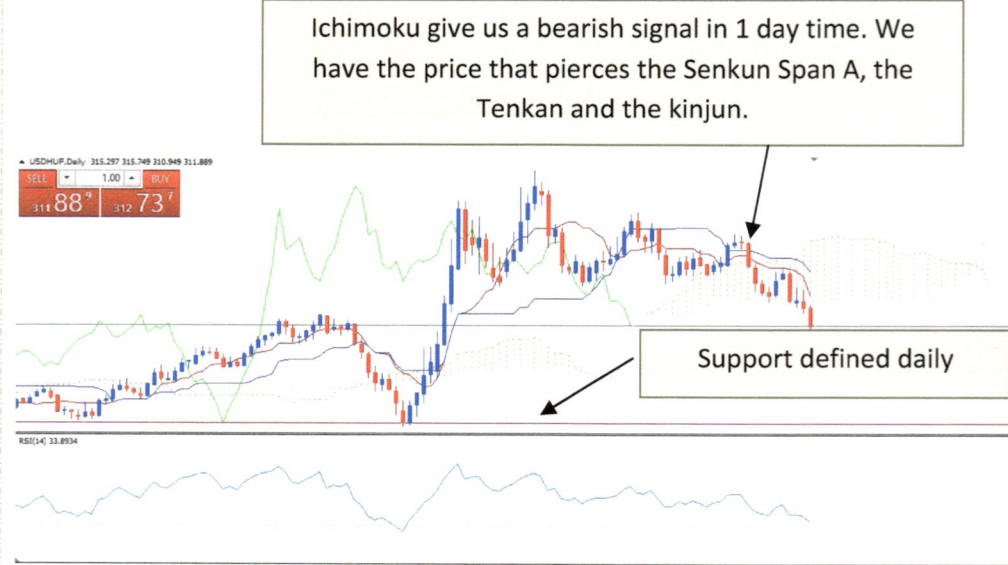

Ichimoku gives us a bearish signal in 4 hour time also (chart below). We have the price breaking through the Tenkan and the Kinjun as well as a cross between the latter two, this confirms the downtrend.

In temporality of 1 hour, we still have stronger bearish signals. We have a cross between Tenkan and Kinjun, a Chikou curve that pierces the Ichimoku cloud and a prize that pierces the Senkun Span B.

The 1 hour support line has been drawn with reference to old prices see chart below

The support plotted on the two charts above, was made on the basis of the old market prices. Looking at the Chikou curve

On the 30 minutes chart we have one final confirmation of the downtrend and we can take a sell position at the best location. The place where the Tenkan and Kinjun crosses and where the price pierces the SSB (Senkoun Span B).

The RSI is above the 30% threshold so there is no fear of trend reversal when taking the sell position. The buy point was here.

We must close the position on the support we had defined in time 1 hour (in red on the chart). We also notice that the RSI at this time has dropped below 30%. So it was one more confirmation to close this position.

> Note : as for the chartist figure. This is a double bottom. We notice that the price hits the same resistances twice and then collapses.

b) <u>Use of moving averages and RSI :</u>

The method consists, as with Ichimoku, of checking the graphs over different temporalities.

To take a buy position on a 30 minutes chart, the 200 period and 50 period averages would need to be below the price, in temporality (1 day; 4 hours and 1 hour). Then for the 30 minutes temporality, it would be necessary that the curve of the average 200 periods is below the price and that the latter intercepts upward the average 50 periods, this by checking the RSI also which must not be in excess purchase (above 70%)

On the contrary, to take a sell position on a chart in 30 minutes. The averages of 200 periods and 50 periods should be above the price, in temporality (1 day, 4 hours, 1 hour). Then for the 30 minutes temporality, it would be necessary that the average 200 periods is above the price and that the price intercepts the average 50 periods downwards and this by checking once again the RSI, which must not be over sale (that is to say less than 30%)

CONCLUSION :

To conclude we will say that the most important element in trading, is to have a trading journal to note down your strategy and follow it to the letter.

There is no need to venture and take a position if we do not have all the indicators that give us the same sell or buy signal and over different timeframes as well.

Risk management also plays an important role. If you are wrong about a buy or a sell position, do not hesitate to stop your loss quickly and if, on the contrary, you are right, do not hesitate to wait until reaching the objective (the defined supports or resistances).

Finally, I would say that you can also complete this training with practice, from a demo account, to also test different leverage effects with a well-defined starting capital.

www.ingramcontent.com/pod-product-compliance
Lightning Source LLC
Chambersburg PA
CBHW040344220526
45473CB00009B/2781